# baby™ POWER™

Maximise your baby's
potential through books

*"I think it is a delightful, well-illustrated guide for helping and also informing parents and carers of young children of the advantages of books and learning."* Bookstart Parent.

# Barrie Wade & Maggie Moore

EGMONT WORLD LIMITED

# ABOUT THE AUTHORS

**Barrie Wade** is Professor of English in Education at the University of Birmingham and, prior to that, he taught in both primary and secondary schools. He has a deep interest in the development of language in young children and in how learning takes place, and he still teaches regularly in schools. He has written books for teachers and more than 100 articles on language and story, special educational needs and language development and is also a widely read author for children, having published poetry, fiction and information books.

**Maggie Moore** is Director of School of Arts and Social Sciences at Newman College, Birmingham and prior to that taught in primary schools and was head of an assessment unit. Her interests lie in psychological aspects of education and literacy and she, too, has contributed extensively in books for teachers in these areas. She is also a fiction writer for children and has developed several wordless picture books for young learners.

### DEDICATION
For Jessica, one of the first Bookstart babies.

B.W.  M.M.

### ACKNOWLEDGEMENTS
The authors would like to acknowledge the help generously given
by parents and their children in the creation of this book.
We should also like to acknowledge the enthusiasm and initiative of
Book Trust, especially Wendy Cooling, and the Unwin Foundation,
especially Raynor Unwin, without whom the pilot project of
Bookstart would never have taken place.

Designed by Anne Sharples
Photography by Steve Gorton and Barrie Wade
Illustrations by Andy Cooke
The Publishers would like to thank:
Simon Connor, Danielle Efstathious, Fisun Efstathious, Mario Efstathious,
Aryana George-Kacou, Shireen Nelson-Williams, Helen Simpson, Jaryn Wright.

Published in Great Britain in 2000 by Egmont World,
an imprint of Egmont Children's Books Limited,
239 Kensington High Street, London. W8 6SA.
Printed in China.
Hardback ISBN 0 7498 4483 3
Paperback ISBN 0 7498 4484 1
A catalogue record for this book is available from the British Library.

# CONTENTS

# INTRODUCTION

### YOUR CHILD NEEDS YOU

This book is for you and your child. You care for your child and your child needs you whether you are Dad or Mum, Grandma, Grandad, Aunty, Uncle or other relative or carer. By *you* we mean all of you who care for infants under school age.

You have an important part to play in talking to your child and introducing your child to books. This book will show you why and how.

Also, this book is for all children under school age, whether babies, toddlers or infants. It's never too soon to take your child into the fun world of books and to start giving your child the advantages that books bring.

### ABOUT BOOKSTART

**Bookstart** *is a Book Trust project first introduced in Birmingham in 1992. Librarians and health visitors worked in liaison to give a Bookstart pack to parents and babies. Librarians constructed the pack, which contained a book, nursery rhyme card, information about book clubs and the local library (with an invitation to join). Health visitors gave the packs to parents and their babies at the 9-month hearing test, explained its purpose and encouraged parents to share the book, and others, with their baby.*

This book is a gateway to the opportunities and pleasure that books bring for both your child and yourself. It is now well known that an early start on books gives children a head start at school. But there's also all the fun of sharing stories, stretching imagination and learning in the quality time you and your child spend together. So have fun, enjoy yourself and see in your own child the amazing difference that sharing books will make.

*Take your child into the fun world of books.*

# 1 □□□□□□

# IT'S NEVER TOO SOON

Not so long ago people thought that they should wait until children went to school before sharing books with them. Somehow parents felt they didn't know enough. Some schools made it worse by telling parents not to interfere. What a waste! Many parents and their children missed out on sharing the fun of books, stories and rhymes and many children struggled later because they had not learned the basic foundations of literacy. They had not learned to concentrate. Nor did they expect to enjoy books. Some children became frustrated learners. Some remained illiterate.

The problem was that sharing books was confused with teaching reading. It may be the school's business to teach reading, but that job is made so much easier if children go to school:

❏ having had stories regularly read to them;
❏ having had chance to talk about stories, pictures and what happens;
❏ knowing and being able to retell familiar stories;
❏ knowing some nursery rhymes;
❏ knowing how a book works (e.g. how to turn the pages, or lift the flaps if it is a flap book);
❏ knowing that books are fun.

*Babies learn how a book works.*

Only you can make sure your child has full access to what books offer and it's never too early to begin.

## YOUR BABY NEEDS YOU

We now know that all babies and toddlers benefit from book sharing with interested adults.

Later sections show what babies can do and how rapid their development is. Again, however, we emphasise your key role in the process. Babies and toddlers learn from the company they keep. The child that nobody talks to learns to keep silent.

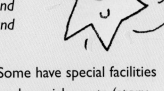

## STAR FACTS

*The majority of Bookstart schemes begin at around 9 months. Professionals, such as health visitors and librarians, recommend this start time.*

❏ Libraries welcome babies. Some have special facilities (e.g. baby changing rooms) and special events (story time for babies or workshops for parents).

❏ Some Bookstart schemes have experimented successfully with babies as young as 5 months. Other people claim that pregnant mums who sing tunes or play cassette tapes of nursery rhymes *before their baby is born* teach their babies rhythm, rhyme, etc. This is difficult to prove, but we reckon it is a good way to relax during pregnancy and also to learn the songs and rhymes that you can use after your baby is born.

The child deprived of books never learns the pleasure, satisfaction and skills that they offer. Your role in book sharing is vital as an interested adult and your child's first teacher. The time you spend is quality time. As such it repays both you and your child in pleasure, satisfaction and later achievement.

## WHEN TO START BOOK SHARING

We recommend you begin when your baby is about 9 months old. By this time you will have established many of the other routines (bathing, feeding, outings, etc.). Your daytime pattern will suggest good times to relax and have fun with books.

You can discuss this start time with your health visitor. She and your local librarian will recommend suitable books. Your local area may already have a Bookstart scheme which offers advice to parents and some free starter books for babies. The organisers of the scheme will also give advice and support.

*Books help children learn to concentrate.*

# 2
□□□□□

# YOUR CHILD, YOUR FAMILY

### NOT JUST FOR CHRISTMAS

**The slogan 'A dog is not just for Christmas' helps to point out the responsibility of pet ownership.**

A new baby demands even more commitment and responsibility, not just for the infant years nor even just for childhood.

Children need time, money and care for all their young, growing lives. You have taken on an important task. But there are compensations. Youngsters are:

- ❏ **fun;**
- ❏ **full of interest;**
- ❏ **deeply satisfying;**
- ❏ **a source of love and fulfilment.**

You help to shape your child in these growing years. You make your child different, an individual.

Every newborn baby is different. Except for identical twins, each infant develops obvious differences. Children differ in height, weight, facial features, etc. What we don't so easily see are the significant differences in personality, character and ways of thinking and feeling that also distinguish all children. Different homes, different cultures, different experiences and contact with different adults produce differences in children, just as important as the physical differences they are born with.

You help to shape these differences and you can have fun and excitement helping your child to learn.

*You can have fun and excitement helping your child to learn.*

## FAMILY SUPPORT

A family gives a child shelter, food and protection. But just as important to the growing child are:

- ❏ love;
- ❏ care;
- ❏ training.

A family gives these too. Some developments of modern living bring advantages for children. For example, shared roles in the modern family allow fathers to enjoy the fun of looking after children. Also, family support and labour-saving devices, plus shorter working hours, allow mothers time to enjoy their children.

Some children have the advantage of a family that includes grandparents, and/or great-grandparents, aunts and uncles, older brothers and sisters as well as parents. All these can play an invaluable part in a child's mental and emotional development, but the advantage disappears if family members are unwilling to take an interest. It's far better for a child to have one parent who is caring and willing to spend quality time helping a child learn, than a whole family of uncommitted, unhelpful relatives.

Three crucial things are necessary for early learning, whether they are provided by a single adult, or by other family members sharing the role. These necessary provisions are given by adults willing to help children learn. They are:

- ❏ time;
- ❏ sharing;
- ❏ praise.

## TIME

Babies and toddlers need time with adults to learn crucial things. One of the most important is the learning of language. Children need adults to **talk to them** so that they have a model of language to imitate. They need adults to **listen to them** so they can see their requests are answered, their needs can be met and they can be understood. All this takes time. Infants learn from regularly recurring patterns. It may take many repetitions over months of "Daddy's coming home" before the youngster experiments with "Daddy home."

Something similar goes on when a child asks for the same bedtime story night after night. Partly this is a need for security. But repetition also provides regularly recurring features of a story to contemplate, learn and continually enjoy.

We need to give children the time to learn – and that means giving them our time.

## SHARING

Giving time to children means sharing something of ourselves, whether we are also sharing in their play, in their talk, in their stories or in their books. This shared, quality time demands our full attention. We can't expect children to learn concentration if we are half-hearted and, for example, watch TV while we share talk or books! Sharing with children means that we give them our undivided attention. But the rewards are huge.

Sharing books with children:

- ❏ **gives pleasure to child and adult;**
- ❏ **develops bonds between child and adult;**
- ❏ **develops a child's language and understanding of the world;**
- ❏ **helps a child settle, concentrate and behave better.**

Interestingly, children's bad behaviour is associated with being lonely, bored and insecure. The interaction of sharing books with adults reduces aggression by giving purpose, point and pleasure.

## PRAISE

Praise is an important ingredient in the learning recipe. It's a bit like the yeast that makes bread rise.

Ask yourself if you like to be praised for something you have done well. Equally, would you like to be continually told off for something you can't do? Anyone told often enough that they are stupid, comes to believe it.

Babies and toddlers are not stupid. In fact, they can learn at a rate that adults cannot match. But they need praise:

*Children learn from the company they keep.*

- ❑ **to mark their achievements;**
- ❑ **to give them confidence;**
- ❑ **to encourage further learning.**

So give praise when babies

- ❑ **hold the book;**
- ❑ **point to pictures;**
- ❑ **try to turn the page;**

and give praise when toddlers

- ❑ **listen attentively;**
- ❑ **try to join in;**
- ❑ **turn the pages.**

**Show** your pleasure and approval. Give a smile as well as giving praise. (*"Well done! Who's a clever girl? You say it well. Good boy. You can join in really well."*)

# 3

□□□□□□

# WHAT BABIES CAN DO

**The full potential of babies to learn from experience has only recently been recognised.**

Our five senses are the ways through which we register experiences and learn from them. Babies are born with these senses in place.

At birth babies can:

| | |
|---|---|
| **SEE** | A newborn infant will screw up its eyes if a bright light is shone. |
| **HEAR** | A baby will react to sounds at birth. Sudden sounds make a baby cry or jerk legs and arms. |
| **TASTE** | Newborns visibly enjoy the taste of milk. |
| **SMELL** | A newborn baby will wrinkle its face if there is a pungent or powerful smell. |
| **TOUCH** | Newborn babies can already grasp a finger and are themselves soothed by cuddling. |

These senses are refined and much learning and development takes place in the first 9 months.

At 9 months old a baby can:

❑ **sit up;**
❑ **use hands to move about on the floor;**
❑ **use hands to pull up to a standing position;**
❑ **hold things with finger and thumb.**

Have you noticed how often infants deliberately drop things for you to pick up and hand back? This is another regularly recurring pattern which helps learning and which is fun – at least for babies!

By 9 months many infants are learning to use their index finger to point.

*He is ready to sit up, hold a book and point to pictures.*

At 9 months a baby is ready to sit up, hold a book and point to pictures.

At 9 months old a baby can:

❏ **focus on objects;**
❏ **concentrate on interesting things.**

By 9 months infants are learning to recognise things and people and can follow movements precisely.

At 9 months a baby is ready to follow the pages of a picture book and to recognise its contents.

At 9 months old a baby can:

❏ **recognise familiar voices;**
❏ **respond to his/her own name, the names of other people, toys, etc.;**
❏ **hear and understand simple instructions and questions.**

By 9 months babies are learning from their interaction with adults. The regularly recurring pattern of feeding means that a baby's mouth will open when food is on the spoon and the adult says "open". "Give Mummy a kiss" will often draw an appropriate response and, "Where's Daddy?" will send the infant's glance to the appropriate person.

At 9 months a baby is ready to follow the regular pattern of a picture book's pages and to respond to the pictures.

At 9 months old a baby can:

❏ **babble and 'talk' to people and him/herself;**
❏ **repeat sounds;**
❏ **try to copy adults.**

By 9 months infants are beginning to experiment with sounds and to use them to make meaning.

At 9 months a baby is ready for the speech practice that sharing books and rhymes gives.

# 4

# HOW STORIES AND BOOKS CAN HELP YOUR BABY

## READING AND STORY

All children enjoy being read to: like us, they enjoy a good story. We are all natural storytellers. Most of our own conversations are narratives with other adults. We tell the story of what has happened to us. We exchange experiences. We are interested in other people's lives. Even gossip is storytelling.

**Both the spoken word and the printed word bring important opportunities for infants and toddlers.**

## TELL ME A STORY

Tellers and listeners make a bond. When we tell stories young children are entertained and learn from the story's content, creativity and expressiveness, as children have done throughout the ages. Listening to stories is a natural process through which youngsters:

- ❏ **stretch their imagination;**
- ❏ **share experiences;**
- ❏ **are entertained;**
- ❏ **are inspired;**
- ❏ **learn.**

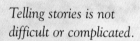

*Telling stories is not difficult or complicated.*

To tell stories is not difficult or complicated. Children love anecdotes. Tales about yourself and familiar relatives are much enjoyed (*"Remember what happened to Daddy when he lost his keys…"*). Folk tales, fairy tales and fables from your particular culture and others are treasured (*"Now this is how the elephant got his trunk. One day…"*). Children particularly love tales which involve themselves (*… "so this is how you fell in the mud."*). These are stories that children will ask for again and again.

## USING BOOKS FOR STORYTELLING

You can also add to your repertoire from the books you and your infant have shared, and you will tell these stories naturally. For example, when you have regularly shared the story of *Goldilocks and the Three Bears* in book form, both you and the child will know the story pretty well. You can then have great fun telling the story using the three powerful aids to storytelling:

**VOICE** try different voices for the three bears;

**FACIAL EXPRESSION** try showing 'too hot' or 'too salty' with facial expressions;

**GESTURE** try showing size and movement with hand gestures.

It is never too soon to begin simple storytelling with your baby. Babies react positively to the strong rhythms of nursery rhymes - which are, of course, stories and songs.

With older children you can make a feature of storytelling. Nothing elaborate is needed. Voice, facial expression and gesture are still the key features. However, to gain attention you might begin with a simple object (e.g. a key or a toy, a picture or puppet, perhaps a photograph of the child as a baby).

Story is a process that young children naturally engage in from the time that they produce their early single words. "Mummy" may mean "Mummy has gone away", "Hello, Mummy, you've come back", or "I want my dinner." Language is thus capable of referring to past and future events as well as those in the immediate present. Stories give children the power to speculate and reflect. They learn to predict possible happenings, as well as shaping events in the past and organising present experiences. Once a child has a story, it exists to be reflected on, reworked, adapted, modified or retold. Encourage this with your child. It is great fun for you too.

## READ ME A BOOK

Sharing a book is fun for both adult and infant. Simple books with clear, bright pictures fascinate babies, as do rhymes and stories. A baby of 9 months or so soon learns:

- ❏ **to concentrate on the sequence of pages;**
- ❏ **to hold the book the right way up;**
- ❏ **to point to pictures;**
- ❏ **to listen attentively;**
- ❏ **to help turn pages.**

As you talk about the pictures (*"Look at the black rabbit. Can you see what big ears it's got?"*) a baby will listen attentively. Much incidental learning takes place this way.

Later you can encourage joining in. *"Can you point to the black rabbit? Where are its ears?"*

Your model of how to hold the book, how to turn pages, to point to pictures, to talk about them, is what counts. Babies learn from the company they keep. You and the book are the baby's company. With practice the infant becomes very good at sharing the book with you.

### FILLING THE GAPS

Later, when the toddler's language is developing, try leaving spaces in a rhyme or familiar phrase for the child to fill.

*"I'll huff and I'll ..... and I'll blow your house ..... ."*
*"Round and round the garden, like a teddy ..... ."*

You will be surprised how quickly children learn to fill the gaps and how much fun this is for both of you.

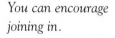

*You can encourage joining in.*

### LEARNING TO PREDICT

As children develop confidence, encourage them to say what they think will happen in a storybook. The title and pictures are important clues. Help children to read the pictures. *"What is the dog doing?" "Where do you think he's going?" "Look, he's fallen in the hole!" "Will he get dirty?" "What will happen when he gets home?"*

As children become more familiar with stories they become better at knowing how stories work. Some of their predictions can be better than the original!

Rhythm and rhyme patterns also help children to make predictions. **Incy Wincy Spider climbed up the water spout, Down came the rain and washed poor spider ....** **Out came the sun** (*"What do you think happens to the rain?"*) **and dried up all the rain.** (*"And what does Incy Wincy Spider do?"*) **So Incy Wincy Spider climbed back again.**

## TALKING ABOUT PICTURES

Centuries ago readings aloud from the Bible and the stained-glass windows depicting scenes that could be talked about were important for a church congregation that were not able to read themselves. Pictures in early children's books have the same function. Repeated reading and talking about the pictures with your infant soon helps him/her to 'read' the pictures and gain information from them. In new books a child will expect the pictures to tell part of the story. Later on the child will be able to retell a familiar story by using the pictures as a guide.

So one of the best things you can do during and after reading the books is to talk about the pictures, helping your child to gain information and strengthen his/her own ability to tell stories.

### STAR FACTS

*As a result of starting to share books with babies at 9 months of age Bookstart families:*

❏ shared books more with their infants;

❏ read more;

❏ enrolled more infants as library members;

❏ bought more books than other families.

# 5

ꗃꗃꗃꗃꗃꗃ

# QUALITY TIME

One of the most important factors influencing the development of infants and toddlers is the quality of their relationship with whoever is caring for them. A warm, loving relationship is worth more than gold. Giving time is more important than giving money.

However, busy adults have lots to do and often put themselves under pressure. This is why quality time is important - for adults as well as children. Positive interaction and learning from those around us are keys to learning.

By quality time we mean giving of oneself fully, responsively, focusing on the child totally. Quality time periods may be relatively short. They also need to fit in with your particular routine. Good times are:

❏ a mid-morning break;
❏ after lunch;
❏ during bath time;
❏ just before bedtime.

Other occasions will present themselves spontaneously.

*Quality time is important – for adults as well as children*

In quality time you:

- ❏ **give emotional support;**
- ❏ **talk with your child;**
- ❏ **build trust;**
- ❏ **help your child's confidence and learning.**

For yourself you:

- ❏ **slow down the pace;**
- ❏ **relax with your child;**
- ❏ **point to pictures;**
- ❏ **listen attentively;**
- ❏ **help turn pages.**

In quality time you build your child's sense of self through:

- ❏ **consistency;**
- ❏ **challenge;**

and sharing books is a central, valuable activity.

## CONSISTENCY

A toddler loves to curl up, to sit on a lap. A warm, soft environment gives the security needed for consolidating learning and for new challenges.

A familiar place (an armchair, a carpeted corner) for sharing books adds to the security, as does the familiar pattern of doing this regularly. So, too, the regular predictable patterns of familiar, well-loved books help to give confidence. Learning is consolidated by constant repetition of known favourite stories and rhymes. Repeated phrases encourage listening, concentration and learning, e.g. *"I'll huff and I'll puff and I'll blow your house down,"*; and *"Humpty Dumpty sat on a wall, Humpty Dumpty had a great fall."*

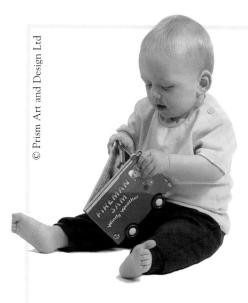

*New books mean the excitement of new learning.*

## CHALLENGE

When your child is secure and confident you can introduce new challenges. These may be in the form of new books from the library or bookshop. New books mean the excitement of new learning and new experiences, but the security and consistency provide bridges to discovery. Your role is to encourage, to support and to provide a model! Soon some of these new books will become favourites too.

## SHARE A BOOK OR CLEAN A ROOM?

Some adults feel guilty if they read themselves. They wrongly think it means wasting time. Clearly a balance needs to be sought between necessary adult tasks and self-improvement. However, children cannot make these choices themselves and book sharing in quality time is necessary for their intellectual and emotional development.

So don't feel guilty about reading - certainly not to your child. It's better to help build your child's future than to worry about chores all the time.

Children enjoy relaxed, easy-going parents, so make some time to relax and to have fun with your child. What works for him or her works for you, so give yourself a break. Give yourself quality time.

## STRENGTHENING THE BOND

The love, time and attention you give in quality time is repaid by the security, affection and comfort felt by your child. Book sharing contributes to confident, happy children and strong bonding between them and the adults who share pleasure with them.

© Mrs Roger Hargreaves

*Book sharing contributes to confident, happy children.*

Bonding is reinforced by:

❏ physical contact (e.g. as you and your child sit comfortably together);

❏ repeated patterns of action (e.g. as you turn pages and talk about familiar pictures);

❏ repeated patterns of words (e.g. the familiar story sequence or rhyme);

❏ comfort and relaxed pleasure (e.g. the soothing rhythm of song, the predictable pattern of rhyme).

So make time for your child and enjoy it!

# 6

□□□□□□

# WHAT PARENTS SAY

**When parents need advice about their children, one of the best places to go to is another parent who has already been through the same stage.**

In this section we give examples of what parents say about children who have had books shared with them since they were babies.

First, Tracey Ebanks talks about her son, Naquarné. Like many parents, Tracey says that she would not have thought of sharing books with her baby if it had not been for the advice and support of her health visitor.

**Baa!** *is Naquarné's favourite book. Now at 10 months he still loves the fluffy sheep.*

> *I always pictured reading to him when he was older, before bedtime when he was old enough to understand - say at school age.*
>
> *To be honest, I didn't think a baby could concentrate on a book. I was amazed at how he watched my hand from the very beginning. He's always learning. He has learned how to hold the book, to turn the page, he points to the picture, he feels soft furry things in books, like* **Baa!***, he lifts flaps. He is learning lots. He's very good with his fingers. He doesn't just hit things. He can point and press things and touch things quite gently.*

Tracey also mentions how books became part of a routine to settle Naquarné.

> *I've had a few problems getting him to sleep at night. Now I give him his last bottle in the bedroom and we look at a book together. Now he is in a routine and he's no problem.*

Tracey is one of many parents who have found the help and support from her local library very useful. Books are expensive, but libraries now positively encourage babies to become members.

*He's a library member already. He can have up to six books now. I became a member too. I've never been one to read, but I read more now. They do a group for babies every Tuesday, with nursery rhymes, and one of the library assistants reads a story. It's really good. He's got lots of favourite books, but he still likes* **Baa!** *- the first book he had.*

Finally, Tracey confirms what we say later in section 8 - that adults themselves profit from sharing books with children.

*I reckon, I've got a lot out of it myself. We sit down together and read together. I'm always rushing about, but I look forward to our time together when we sit together. We really get to know each other. It's that quiet time - no television on, no noise - it makes me relaxed. It relaxes both of us.*

Dads, grandads, older brothers and uncles have an important part to play in book sharing. It is important to show that reading is fun for male and female members of the family.

*Naquarné has learned to hold the book and lift the flaps.*

BAA! © Treehouse Children's Books Ltd. Illustrations © Steve Cox

23

Mr Bhatt shared books with his young daughter from the age of 3 or 4 months and, like every other parent, wants to do the best he can for his child.

*I'm sure it works, even from 3 or 4 months old, when she got her first book, but she seems to be getting on very well. We are always wanting to improve on what we are doing. We just want the best for her.*

She is now 15 months old and a library member.

*We always got books from the library for her. She'll open books, turn the pages and she will recognise things from books. She has her favourite words. She will say, "That's a car." Her favourite word is "star". She has stars on the ceiling in her bedroom, which are luminous, and "star" was the first word that she said. I hope she is a star in the classroom when she grows up!*

*My wife went to the library yesterday afternoon, to a gathering with babies and toddlers. It was the first time she had been to this group and she enjoyed her time there. She enjoyed it yesterday and she will go back again. I want to take her to the library because eventually she will want to go there herself. If you direct a child that way, that's where she'll want to go.*

Mr Bhatt also emphasises the importance and pleasure of regular book sharing sessions. He shares these with his wife, but very much enjoys being involved himself.

*I'm not saying I sit down every night with her, but I take the opportunity when there's a convenient time. I usually take her away from the sitting-room because that is where the television is and I go through a few books with her. We really enjoy it.*

Dominic (24 months) has his favourite books and can point out items that interest him.

Jude Glynn is one of many parents who now benefit from Bookstart, the project which encourages parents to share books with their babies from 8 or 9 months of age. Jude first received a free book for Dominic when she took him for his hearing check at the age of 9 months. Included in the pack was a poem card, poster, information about libraries, etc. Since these early days Jude and her husband have found time every day to share books with their son, so that now it is a routine.

*I make sure we look at books last thing at night with Dominic.*

**Say Goodnight** *was Dominic's first book. He still enjoys sharing it with Mum.*

All children have their favourite books, and often these date from their early experiences. This is true of Dominic, because the first free book he received at 9 months old is still a favourite at 24 months.

*The book he got from Bookstart was the first book Dominic got that was just his. We've got a lot of books that have been bought for his older sisters. Now he's had more books bought for him. We are lucky that relatives buy him books, but* **Say Goodnight** *is still one of his favourites.*

Most babies will explore books to begin with by putting them to their mouths. Dominic did this at first, but he soon learned what a book is for.

*He took* **Say Goodnight** *to his grandma's for the weekend. It's complete with teeth-marks, but it's still OK. He's good with books.*

Jayne Turner tells how she was taken by surprise at what her young baby could do before 6 months of age. Jayne received free books via her health visitor when Zoë was only 4 months. She began showing books to Zoë at this time and was amazed that it soon led to learning.

*Zoë, now aged 3, 'teaches' her Mum to count the stars!*

*We got a Bookstart pack from the health visitor really early when Zoë was just over 4 months. I would never have dreamt that a young baby would sit with me and look at pictures. At first you felt a bit silly because you were doing all the talking and half the time feeding her, but after a few weeks she was putting her hand out to the books and, instead of me turning the pages, she was trying to turn them. She was only 6 months. Right from go, when she started holding a book herself, she has never had it the wrong way round. Now she can concentrate on books for a long time. She is 3 now and she has her own writing books which she tries to write in. She's only just 3.*

Zoë may be only just 3, but she is well on the way to laying the foundations for much future learning, and she also has lots of fun.

*She can count very well and she has learned that from books. We've always said, "How many rabbits? How many balls?" We count the balloons in her* **Thomas the Tank Engine** *book. She has just been teaching me to count the stars in one of her books! She now knows all the shapes - triangle, star, circle, square, and all the colours.*

Zoë has her own stack of books and loves playing at being a bookshop owner. She has a little till and a barcode reader. Of course, she knows where to find the barcode on each book. The books are carefully stacked in Zoë's bookshop and Jayne makes the point that, despite her own earlier misgivings, Zoë has always treated books carefully.

The children climbed into the carriage for the party.

The driver said it was the nicest birthday he had ever had.

*I expected to have them shredded. If it wasn't in her mouth, I expected them to be ripped up. But Zoë never put them to her mouth. She treated them well from the start. It surprised me, I must admit. I can't think of any book that she has ever damaged. You go into a friend's house, where they haven't had books from babies. You see books there torn and with the pages out. They don't know what to do with them.*

*Zoë can count the balloons.*

These parents clearly see the advantages of early book sharing with babies. They are the best judges of their own children, because they have shared, as close observers, in their children's development. There is much encouragement in what they say and tremendous opportunities for other adults and babies.

*Zoë has her own play bookshop complete with barcode reader and till.*

# 7

# WHAT CHILDREN GAIN FROM SHARING BOOKS

## OPERATING AT A HIGHER LEVEL

Books give children more than just facts or the chance to be literate. Books encourage children to see that other people have different ways of thinking and acting. In this way they help children to know more about themselves and others and to predict and explain people's actions.

The psychologist, Lev Vygotsky, once explained it this way:

*"Sharing books with adults enables children to operate at a higher level than they could on their own."*

## FROM THE BEGINNING

You help your baby from the beginning by sharing books. These sharing sessions lead to learning and co-operating at a higher level.

*The child learns to recognise objects and to share in talk about them.*

**LOOKING AT PICTURES** together may seem to be a simple activity, but your baby is learning important concepts of number, colour, shape and size. The young child learns that a dog, for example, can be represented by a picture. The child learns to recognise objects and to share in talk about them.

**LISTENING TO STORIES** over again may seem simple repetition, but it is a powerful force for learning. Your baby learns to listen and to concentrate. Toddlers who have listened to stories become familiar with patterns of narrative and understand sequence and prediction. Later a young child will discover more about print - that the words of text represent the story; that books and text go from left to right. This natural learning underpins later reading activity.

**JOINING IN** with a rhyme or story may seem a simple imitation, but it signifies knowledge of how books work and familiarity with pattern. The ability to join in signals success to you and your child and leads to confidence, self-reliance and high self-esteem.

## ROCK BABY TEDDY

What we have said in this section is illustrated neatly by Imogen, a toddler aged 24 months. She has been put to sleep in her cot, but instead, like most toddlers, chatters to herself first.* She is alone, except for her teddy bear, and this is what she says. Remember, the transcript of the tape-recording is speech, not writing.

*Laughses (Laughs) Laughs… I… Um out Teddy um out… m…Mout fing… Wing.. Ling look… Ting… Kfing look… Fwing look Teddy… Dont bwing… Bwing… Good Teddy… Up… Good Teddy… Good Teddy… Good Teddy… Rock baby down the top Teddy… Down y Teddy… Talk… Now… Rock baby down a top fall… Rock baby on a tee top will… Down come baby fell will.*

wing   ling look   ting   kfing look
fwing   look   Teddy

To begin with, this is surprisingly fluent and extensive for 24 months of age. Yet those children who are regularly talked to will use language confidently like this. Clearly Imogen has been talked to. Did you notice how she seems to be talking to her teddy in the same way as an adult has talked to her (repeating praise)? *"Good Teddy, Good Teddy, Good Teddy."* Clearly an adult has given her similar encouragement, or she could not do this. She also seems to be practising sounds and words. *"Fing Wing Ling Ting Kfing Fwing."* Is it the word "swing" she is trying to say? *"Rock Baby down the top Teddy, Rock Baby down a top fall, Rock Baby on a top will"* and *"Down come baby fell will"* are her attempts at the words of the nursery rhyme, e.g. *"Rock-a-bye Baby on a tree top"* and *"Down will come Baby, cradle and all."* What is amazing is that Imogen's attempts follow the tune of the rhyme as it had previously been sung to her.

Imogen could not have done any of this without the quality time spent with adults and there are plenty of children who arrive at school age with none of these skills in place. Imogen has learned from **Rhyme, Rhythm and Repetition** - the *Three Rs* most important in early learning.

*Sharing books develops learning potential.*

It would be interesting to know if Imogen's learning potential is similar to other children who receive an early start with books. Luckily we can answer that question.

We were involved with the first Book Trust experiment in Britain when health visitors gave free children's books to families with 9-month-old children. So impressed were we with the early results that, over the years, we ran conferences and encouraged more projects to begin.

Soon many thousands of families were involved and today there is a national Bookstart organisation and a national sponsor to provide funding.

We also kept track of the families in the first experiment. Recently, their children reached school age (5), so we were able to compare them with a similar group who had not received a Bookstart pack at 9 months.

We used results of Baseline tests given by teachers when children have settled down in their first schools. We did this so that there should not be any bias in the findings. None of the teachers knew which children had been involved as babies in Bookstart.

Results were clear-cut. There were three baseline scores in English (Speaking and Listening, Reading and Writing) and a maximum of 9 points could be scored. *Figure 1* shows the average score (mean) of Bookstart children (almost 4.6) compared with the group who had not received books at 9 months (less than 3.6).

*FIG. 1*

## BOOKSTART CHILDREN - COMPARISON GROUP - ENGLISH BASELINE SCORES

COMPARISON                    BOOKSTART

This is a large and significant difference, showing that the Bookstart group as a whole had the foundations of literacy more securely in place than the comparison group.

31

What was surprising was that the three scores for mathematics produced results almost as decisive.

*FIG. 2*

## BOOKSTART CHILDREN - COMPARISON GROUP - MATHEMATICS BASELINE SCORES

COMPARISON                                    BOOKSTART

This shows the average score for mathematics (mean) of Bookstart children (above 4.4) compared with the group who had not received books at 9 months (about 3.6).

*An early start with books helps children prepare for school.*

Taken together these findings show that the Bookstart group, who had all received the Bookstart pack in infancy, had been better prepared for school by their early childhood experiences.

We said that the results in mathematics surprised us at first, but there are likely reasons for the superiority of Bookstart children.

32

Firstly, many children's books focus on number and sequence, e.g. *Three Bears* and *Ten, Nine, Eight*. Then, too, early children's books contain number rhymes, e.g., *Five Little Ducks*, *Ten in a Bed* and *One, Two Three, Four, Five, Once I Caught a Fish Alive*. Repeated pleasurable practice with rhymes and counting when sharing books is likely to make number learning interesting and effective.

A second possibility is that regular acts of book sharing in the pre-school years encourage attention and concentration. Book sharing provides pleasurable and purposeful quality time for both infants and adults and we know that it is easier to concentrate if activities are purposeful.

So the quality time you spend sharing books with your child is likely to have a significant effect on your child's future success as well as on the kind of person your child becomes.

*Books enable your child to experiment safely with feelings and ideas.*

## A QUALITY KIND OF PERSON

We have outlined the educational value of book sharing and the advantages of bonding that result from quality time you spend with your child. We shouldn't forget the other personal outcomes from book sharing which help make individuals sensible, feeling human beings with secure values.

From the very beginning your baby will share in the construction of stories, enjoying and gaining benefits from this creative process. In sharing a book with you, your child puts him or herself in the shoes of characters in the story. Books enable your child to experiment safely (at one remove, as it were) with feelings and ideas.

Book sharing helps your child:

- ❏ to feel how others feel;
- ❏ to extend his/her world;
- ❏ to widen his/her experience;
- ❏ to develop understanding of others;
- ❏ to deepen understanding of self.

**STAR FACTS**

❏ *Children who engage in sharing books and reading activities at home pay more attention and concentrate more at school.*

The advantages to your child are enormous. Only you, with the help of books, can help your child reach full potential.

# 8

# WHAT'S IN IT FOR ME?

This section spells out the considerable advantages for children when, from babyhood, they share books with adults. You may have been thinking about what's in it for you, remembering that a regular time commitment is demanded. Well, first, there are lots of indirect benefits - feeling you have done the right thing and given your child the best possible chances in life, for example.

We can think of five major advantages for you. Maybe you will think of some more.

## BENEFITS FROM BETTER ACHIEVEMENT

We know that regular book sharing will lay the foundations of literacy for your child. This should mean fewer learning difficulties when your child starts school. The time you spend with your child will result in better concentration later in school and fewer problems for you to deal with.

## BENEFITS FROM QUALITY TIME

You, as well as your child, benefit from the quality time you set aside each day. In a busy sea of work, islands of relaxation are as important to you as to your child.

The warm closeness of contact, the quiet concentration and the repeated patterns of book sharing reduce stress and help you relax.

## BENEFITS FROM PLEASURE AND SATISFACTION

You will have fun sharing books with your child. Parents tell us how much pleasure they have even in their first ventures with 9-month-old babies. A pleasure shared is a pleasure more than doubled. The fun that infants have with books is infectious and will involve you too.

*In a busy sea of work, islands of relaxation are as important to you as to your child.*

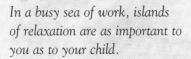

## BENEFITS FROM THE CHANCE TO OBSERVE THE 'MIRACLE' OF INFANT LEARNING

Your baby will learn fast in your company. Book sharing in quality time gives the chance to observe the amazing development of language. It really is remarkable how quickly infants learn to point to pictures, turn pages, chuckle with delight, know when to lift a flap. There is immense joy when a child fills a rhyme gap for the first time, learns a chorus, points out a word - all without being systematically taught.

## BENEFITS FROM THE ACT OF READING

It is interesting that some 'illiterate' parents learn to crack the code of reading only after they have their own children. Sharing books, talking about pictures and observing print are starters for both children and adults. Other parents, who may have drifted away from books themselves, find renewed pleasure in their own reading, having returned to it via the fun of book sharing with their children. However, the books you share with your child will also bring you pleasure. We live in a golden age of children's literature with varied, high-quality books for babies that are not babyish. Many children's books are cleverly written, brilliantly illustrated, deal with important issues and are deeply satisfying. They provide a rich banquet for you and your child to taste together.

## 'DIFFICULT' CHILDREN

As well as the above benefits there is one more which applies to some parents all of the time and all parents some of the time!

All children have times when they don't concentrate, don't listen and don't behave well. However, some infants and toddlers are overactive, impulsive and easily distracted even when they are doing things they enjoy.

You will need lots of patience and calm to deal with such a child, but sharing books, because of the relaxation, contact and repetitive pattern that we've already explained, can be a big help.

A while ago we received this letter from a parent who found book sharing the key for herself and her child.

*Dear Dr Wade*

*I was very interested to read of your findings re: Bookstart, in the education section of the Independent. My daughter, Lucy, was a very difficult baby as she cried almost continually from birth. In desperation, when she was a few weeks old, we looked at books together and I read extensively to her. It was a brief respite from the crying - she was mesmerized. Her love of books grew over the years and she was inconsolable if bedtime stories were missed (they rarely were!). She has gone from strength to strength. Her spelling is excellent. Over the years of spelling tests, she has only once misspelt a word. I'm proud to tell you that at the age of eight, she felt confident enough to attempt* **Great Expectations** *by Charles Dickens. I am certain that early contact with books can only benefit all children.*

*Yours faithfully,*
*Sue Parry*

At some time you have probably been at your wits' end, trying to settle your child and trying to keep cool and calm. Such times recur, so why not try sharing a book?

The following pointers may also be useful:

- ❏ have special book-sharing times in the day, but be prepared to create another as a 'treat';
- ❏ remove distractions – switch off the TV;
- ❏ use physical contact, cradling, touching hands on hands to achieve control, to settle and gain attention;
- ❏ use eye contact to ensure your child is listening;
- ❏ ask questions and listen to your child (*"What do you think the wolf will do now?"*);
- ❏ have a variety of books and give your child a choice (*"Do you want Peter Rabbit or Mr Messy?"*);
- ❏ deflect annoying behaviour rather than confronting it (*"Oh look what she's doing on this page?"*);
- ❏ give praise as soon as your child shows appropriate behaviour. (*"You really hold the book nicely. You **are** clever at turning over"*).

We don't say sharing a book will solve all of your problems, but it will solve some of them, some of the time. So, that's another great advantage to you and one you can use for many years.

*Anytime is a good time for enjoying books.*

37

# 9

# BOOKS FOR BABIES

We referred earlier to the golden age of literature in which we live. The range of books available for children is sometimes bewildering and we sometimes aren't sure of the best books to share with our children, or the best ways in which to share them. The important thing to remember when sharing is that there is no best way, and that you will find *your* way to stimulate your child's development, enjoyment and a love of books to last through to school age and beyond.

We know that books can be expensive, but if you and your baby join your local library you can have access to a wide range of books. You will probably find that your baby quickly finds a favourite book which you will either have to renew regularly or go out and buy! Many bookshops now have a good stock of books for babies.

## WHAT TO LOOK FOR IN A BOOK

**Books for babies need to be sturdy!** There are many board books available. Board books are easy for any child to turn the pages as the pages are easier to grasp. Don't worry if at first your baby puts his or her mouth to the book. This is a way in which very young children explore and learn about their world and about the objects in it. Library staff also understand this; the majority of libraries do not have fines for the under-5s, even if books are damaged.

**Books for babies need to be taken anywhere.** Smaller books e.g. *Numbers Teething Ring book*, and *Rocking Rattle book*, shown left, are ideal. They are easy to carry around in the carry-cot or buggy and can be held by your baby very easily.

**Books for babies need to be bright and colourful.** Bright colours attract your baby's attention and encourage your baby to focus and concentrate on the book.

**Books for babies don't always need to have words.** There are many wordless picture books for babies and older children. This gives you chance to make your own story with your baby.

## USING AND CHOOSING BOOKS

Here are some ways in which you could share books with your child, from 9 months to school age. There will, of course, be other ideas that you will have that will be appropriate for you and your child. The important thing is for both of you to enjoy the activity, so sit back and relax and take the time to share.

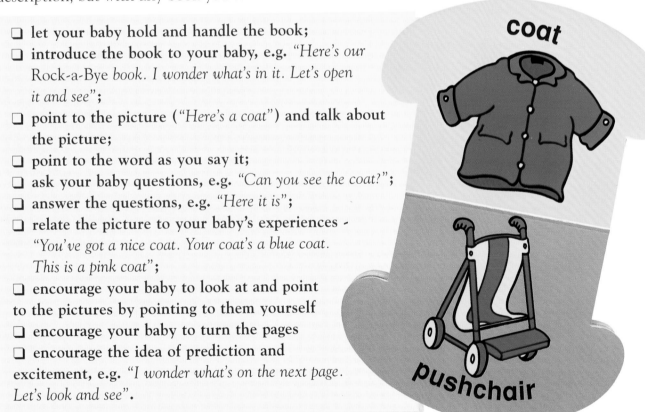

Whichever type of book you share with your baby, there are a number of things you can do. We will use *Rock-a-Bye Words* (Jenny Tulip) as an illustration. This particular book has brightly coloured pages with a one-word description, but with any book you can:

- ❑ **let your baby hold and handle the book;**
- ❑ **introduce the book to your baby, e.g.** *"Here's our Rock-a-Bye book. I wonder what's in it. Let's open it and see"*;
- ❑ **point to the picture** (*"Here's a coat"*) **and talk about the picture;**
- ❑ **point to the word as you say it;**
- ❑ **ask your baby questions, e.g.** *"Can you see the coat?"*;
- ❑ **answer the questions, e.g.** *"Here it is"*;
- ❑ **relate the picture to your baby's experiences -** *"You've got a nice coat. Your coat's a blue coat. This is a pink coat"*;
- ❑ **encourage your baby to look at and point to the pictures by pointing to them yourself**
- ❑ **encourage your baby to turn the pages**
- ❑ **encourage the idea of prediction and excitement, e.g.** *"I wonder what's on the next page. Let's look and see"*.

Your baby can also play with Rock-a-Bye Words by making the book rock before opening and turning the pages.

**Don't worry** if your baby does not always respond to your requests. The sound of your voice, encouragement and the pleasure of the experience are all helpful. A young baby will not be able to answer your questions, or make predictions, but as you continue to use and model these techniques you *will* find your baby beginning to respond. Share your delight as your baby does so and praise your baby.

## BOARD BOOKS

These are sturdy and will probably stand up to quite a lot of mouth contact. Early books for babies should not have sharp corners. The books are usually very colourful with one word or one phrase per page. This lets you talk about the picture, as well as saying the word on the page.

*Numbers* by Simon Abbott is a board book.

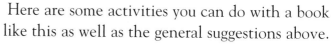

Here are some activities you can do with a book like this as well as the general suggestions above.

❑ **introduce the book, e.g.** *"Here's our counting book, 1, 2, 3, 4, 5"*;
❑ **talk about the animal(s) in the picture;**
❑ **talk about the colours;**
❑ **count the animals in the picture and point to the animals as you are counting, e.g.** *"1, 2, 3, hippos. There are three hippos"*;
❑ **talk about numbers, e.g.** *"How many hands/fingers/toes have you got?"* **Count them out loud;**
❑ **this book has a vine growing across every page. Trace this from left to right as you talk about the book; this will (eventually) encourage your baby to follow words from left to right;**
❑ **reinforce the book sharing with number rhymes that you know, e.g.** *"One, two ,three, four, five, Johnny caught a fish alive. Six, seven, eight, nine, ten, then he let it go again"* **counting fingers or toes as you do so; or,** *"Down at the bottom of the deep blue sea, catching fishes ONE, TWO, THREE"* **and lifting your baby as you count.**

**Follow the Line** (from the **Baby Power** series) has grooves cut into the pages which children can follow with their fingers.

❑ **read the rhyme, and then say,** *"If you move your finger along this line you can show the car where to go,"* **and** *"What sound do you think the car makes?"* **and** *"We like going out in the car, don't we?"*

## FLAP BOOKS

Flap books encourage children to explore and predict.

**Where's Spot?** by Eric Hill has been a favourite book for children for many years. It is a simple 'lift-the-flap book' which you and your baby can enjoy together on many different occasions.

You can:

❑ **talk about the first pages in the book, e.g.** *"There's Spot's mum. She's looking for Spot. What is she saying?"* **then read the text;**

❑ **after reading the first page you can point to the bowls of food,** *"There's Spot's bowl and there's Sally's bowl. Sally is Spot's mum"*;

❑ **read the question on each page and ask** *"Shall we see?"* **before opening the flap;**

❑ **help your baby to turn the pages and open the flaps;**

❑ **read** *"No"* **in a dramatic voice and say** *"It's a bear/ snake" etc.*;

❑ **talk about the animals in the illustrations (especially if your baby has a similar toy);**

❑ **when your child is older, and after much rereading, encourage your child to ask the questions and supply the answers;**

❑ **play the Where's Spot? game with one of your baby's toys, e.g.** *"Where's Teddy? Is he under the chair? No. Is he in the box?" etc.*

© Eric Hill

© NEXT PLC

## NOVELTY CLOTH BOOKS

Books made of cloth are very easy for your baby to handle. This **Play and Learn Nursery Rhymes** book by NEXT contains ten well-known nursery rhymes with opportunities for different activities for you and your child to share. There are lots of things for your baby or young child to manipulate; there is something on every page to pull, stick or move and many different textures to feel:

❑ let your baby explore the book by turning the pages and feeling the different textures;

❑ read the cover page and play the action rhyme 'Round and round the garden like a teddy bear' on your baby's hand;

❑ guide your baby's hand and play the action rhyme with the teddy bears on the cover;

❑ encourage your baby to open the book (it has a Velcro fastening so your baby might need some help);

❑ read and sing the nursery rhyme (e.g. Jack and Jill). Take the picture of Jack and Jill and place them on the Velcro steps for going up the hill and falling down;

❑ run your finger under the text as you read the nursery rhymes;

❑ ask and answer the questions that are on some of the pages, e.g. Baa Baa Black Sheep: *"How many bags are there?"* and count the bags, *"One, two, three. There are three bags"*;

❑ encourage your baby to find Little Bo-Peep's sheep by pulling down the flap (your baby will be able to do this without your help very quickly!);

❑ encourage your baby to scare Miss Muffet with the spider;

❑ point to other features on the page, e.g. the stars, clocks.

© NEXT PLC

FOOTNOTE* This book is no longer available from NEXT.

*Hide and Seek* (Ragdoll Productions) is a concertina rag book with a simple story line of children playing hide and seek. It also has flaps to lift and pockets to explore:

❑ encourage your baby to lift the flaps to find the children and to turn the pages;

❑ read the story to your baby, pointing to the words as you read them;

❑ use different voices for the characters and make your baby laugh;

❑ be surprised when the donkey is behind the curtain, etc.;

❑ play hide and seek or peek-a-boo with your baby.

© Ragdoll Productions (UK) Ltd.

## WORDLESS BOOKS

Wordless books can be a great challenge for you, but also lots of fun. You can interpret the illustrations in your own way and no one can say that you are wrong.

*Miffy's Dream* by Dick Bruna features a baby rabbit:

❑ tell the story as you imagine it;

❑ point to the illustrations as you are telling the story;

❑ suggest what Miffy might be thinking alone or when meeting the other baby rabbit;

❑ encourage the beginnings of prediction, e.g. *"I wonder what they will do next. Will they …"*;

❑ respond to your own predictions, e.g. *"Yes, we were right"*;

❑ ask what the rabbits are doing (don't be afraid to answer your own questions).

© Mercis Publishing BV

# 10
□□□□□□

# THE GROWING CHILD

As your child develops, so does the ability to respond to language, answer your questions, sustain a conversation, join in with story and make predictions about what is going to happen. Your child will understand more about numbers, colours, stories and characters and their feelings. As you talk to your child about the book you are sharing and reading, your child will be able to respond and make suggestions as to what is happening, or what might be happening, particularly when you have encouraged this from the very beginning. Your child might also be able to recognise some simple words and point to the words as you are reading.

It is important to talk about experiences which your child may have had which are similar to those in the book, for example, in *I Like It When...* by Mary Muphy. You can talk about what your child likes and whether this is the same as in the book.

Your child may also have favourite books from babyhood that are still brought to book-sharing times. This is fine. We all love re-reading our favourite books. At the same time, though, introduce your child to other books. For toddlers and infants you will have a wonderful store of story books and information books to choose from. There is still a wide range of wordless books for you to share with your child, although as your child gets older, you might also encourage your child to tell you the story of the pictures, rather than you doing it all the time. This encourages your child to practise the art of sequencing in story.

*As your child develops, so does the ability to join in and make predictions.*

As your child grows older you can add to the suggestions made earlier for book sharing. For example, you can:

❏ introduce the book to your child. Read the title. Show who has written the book;

❏ you may have already read books by the same author. This will give you the opportunity to say, *"Here's another book by … Do you remember the book …"*;

❏ read the title page and ask your child what the book might be about. This encourages your child to make predictions about the story;

❏ read the text and trace the direction of the words as you read them;

❏ read the text and show how it relates to the pictures;

❏ point to any word bubbles in the book and take turns with your child to say the spoken words;

❏ read through the entire story;

❏ as you read the book for the second/third time (or more) encourage your child to join in with parts of the story that can be remembered;

❏ leave spaces when you are reading so that your child can supply the missing word;

❏ relate the story to your child's own experiences;

❏ use different voices for the characters;

❏ use your best story-telling voice;

❏ be prepared to read, and re-read all of these books many times.

*Favourite books from babyhood are still brought to book sharing times. This is fine.*

**STAR FACTS**

*When Bookstart children were 3 years old:*

❏ 100% showed a keen interest in their book.

❏ 68% pointed frequently to the text.

❏ 54% frequently tried to turn the page.

❏ 82% frequently joined in with the story.

❏ 61% frequently asked questions.

❏ 72% answered questions frequently.

© Melanie Walsh 1997

***Do Monkeys Tweet?*** by Melanie Welsh is a question and answer book that you and your child can have fun with.

It asks lots of silly questions and then provides the answers over the page:

❏ read one page, e.g. "Do horses bark?" Encourage your child to answer;
❏ Ask *"What does bark?"* before turning the page to see if your child is right;
❏ read the response and encourage your child to join in;
❏ read the noises the animal makes and encourage your child to join in;
❏ if you have animals, or know someone who does, talk about them to let your child bring his/her experience to the story;
❏ talk about the animals in the book and the range of things that they can do;
❏ make up your own questions about the animals in the book.

***I Like It When...*** by Mary Murphy is a simple book which is a series of statements about what the character, Baby Penguin, likes.

❏ read the text and relate to the pictures, e.g. *"I like it when you hold my hand."* **You can ask your child** whether it is something that is liked. You can say that you like it too;
❏ point to the word bubbles in the book and take turns to say the spoken words;
❏ take time to talk about what you and your child like best.

© Mary Murphy 1997

*I Wish I Were a Dog* by Lydia Monks provides many opportunities to talk about the illustrations.

This page shows numerous ways in which dogs can play in the park.

❏ ask your child to point out what the dogs are doing in the park;
❏ talk about the dogs you have seen when you were out;
❏ talk about what your child can do and what your child would like to do.

© Lydia Monks 1998

*Mr Messy* by Roger Hargreaves is a full length story which needs a settled period of uninterrupted time to read:

❏ talk about the messy house;
❏ as you read the book for the second/third time (or more) encourage your child to join in with parts of the story that can be remembered;
❏ ask your child to find Mr Messy's name on the title page, or in the book;
❏ use different voices for the characters;
❏ use your best story telling voice,
e.g. *Mr Neat hoed*
*and mowed*
*and pruned*
*and snipped*
*and clipped*
*and cleared*
*and dug.*

© Mrs Roger Hargreaves

These are only suggestions. As we said earlier, do what you and your child feel comfortable with. Whatever you and your child do with a book, make it pleasurable so that both of you enjoy the book sharing sessions.

# A FINAL WORD

**You have a most important role to play in providing your child with the best opportunities for learning and development which will help to shape your child's future.**

We have shown that sharing books together has many advantages for promoting such opportunities. By sharing books you can be confident that your child will have the foundations which are crucial to successful learning, for example, concentration and enthusiasm. In addition, you will have helped your child to develop the attitudes and skills that lead to successful reading. Some of these are enjoyment, confidence, knowledge of stories, knowing how to turn the pages of a book, being able to focus on print, knowing which way the print goes across the page and being able to work out what comes next. If you have shared rhymes together your child will also be able to play word games. Your child should have a flying start when entering school.

We have given you some practical ideas on how to share books with your child. All you have to do now is to find a comfortable place, choose a relaxing time, get your favourite books and share in a pleasurable and purposeful activity.

*Share in a pleasurable and purposeful activity.*

For further information about Bookstart contact:
Book Trust,
Book House,
45 East Hill,
London, SW18 2QZ.
Tel. 0181 516 2977